Three Witnesses

THE FIRST WITNESS:

JOHN HUS (1373-1415)

The Moravian movement began with John Hus. He is considered by many historians to have been the first true reformer of the church, preceding Martin Luther by a century. He was also one of the most extraordinary preachers in church history. His challenge to the oppressive religious systems of his time hit Europe like a great spiritual earthquake. Refusing to compromise his convictions, Hus was burned at the stake as a heretic in 1415. In his day, that was the price for challenging the Roman church.

Church officials were convinced that Hus' message would die with him. To their dismay, his heroic death only fanned the flames his message had ignited. Truth is more powerful than death, and persecution only scatters the seeds of truth like the wind. Before he died, Hus prophesied that the message of liberty and spiritual reform would be "a hidden seed" falling into the ground and dying for a season, but one day it would sprout and bear much fruit.

Indeed this seed has sprouted again and again, bearing more fruit than he probably ever dreamed. But before it could sprout, it would be carried in the hearts of great saints who watched over it until the right time. One of the most notable of these who followed in Hus' spiritual lineage was Jon Amos Comenius.

THE SECOND WITNESS:

JON AMOS COMENIUS (1592-1671)

Jon Amos Comenius could be included on a short list of those who have had the most impact on the modern world. He is recognized as the father of modern education, and is still considered by many to be the greatest genius to ever work in that field. His contribution to the science of learning can be traced as a primary cause for the great increase of knowledge that has been the hallmark of the past few centuries. What is not always remembered about him is that his great impact on the march of civilization was the result of his relentless passion to know the Son of God.

Comenius was born in Bohemia (now Czechoslovakia) in 1592. He was so quiet and shy that he was thought to be slightly retarded. However, there were deeper influences on him than were apparent. Born into the Moravian evangelical movement, he was touched early by a profound love for the Savior.

Jon Amos hated his school and was therefore a slow learner. He suffered at the hands of cruel and thoughtless teachers. Later he would call his contemporary schools "slaughterhouses of the mind." He believed that the schools were to blame for causing most children to hate books and literature. Even so, he persevered until he was able to attend the Calvinist University at Herborn. In 1614 he became a teacher at a Moravian school in Prerau. It was there that he introduced the new teaching methods that would change the world.

The fuel that propelled Comenius' quest for knowledge was the belief that because all things were made through Christ and for Him, Christ could be seen in everything (Colossians 1:16). He contended that all true knowledge would reveal the glory of the Christ, declaring that "nature is God's second book." This passion became so contagious that much of the civilized world would be touched by it. Not only did he give birth to modern education, but some of the great revivals over the next four centuries could trace their origins to the seeds sown by this one man.

In 1618 Comenius became the pastor of a Moravian congregation in Fulneck, a position which included being in charge of its school. Soon the school at Fulneck became known throughout Moravia. It was during this time that he began to write extensively. However, dark clouds were gathering over Europe that would radically alter the direction of Comenius' life as the Thirty Years War began to unfold in such a way that his work was often disrupted.

In 1620 the Catholics prevailed at the Battle of the White Mountain, and Moravia officially became Catholic. Comenius was told that he could retain his school on the condition of renouncing his Moravian convictions. He refused and consequently lost not only the school, but also his precious library and all of his writings. When murder, violence and hunger reduced the population of Moravia from three million to one million, Comenius lost his wife and only child as well.

Having endured the worst tragedy that a loving husband and father could suffer, Comenius determined not to look down but up. He felt that he now understood even more what a great sacrifice the Father had made in giving His Son for the sins of the world. He also knew more acutely how desperately this fallen world needed the Savior. Comenius resolved to do all that he could to reveal Him.

In 1624 Jon Amos, the ever faithful pastor, led a small band of exiles out of their native land to seek a safe haven. For the rest of his life, he remained a refugee. Warfare repeatedly erupted around him, always in such a way as to destroy much of his work. Time after time he was driven from his home just when it seemed that the roots he was putting down were beginning to bear fruit. Even through such a remarkable and recurring onslaught, this humble pastor and school teacher never became discouraged. Each time calamity struck, he would just formulate an even greater plan to be implemented at his next destination. He was determined to see the world illuminated with the glory of the Son of God, and he viewed education as a means to this end.

THE PROPHECY

When Comenius and the little band of exiles first left Moravia, he gave a remarkable prophecy. He told his followers that the "hidden seed" John Hus had spoken of would grow and bear fruit *in a hundred years time*. Hus' prophecy had been kept alive in the hearts of the Moravians for more than two hundred years, and Comenius declared that in another century it would finally sprout.

To our modern church so often bound by the "tyranny of the immediate," a prophesy that the hope of revival would not be fulfilled for another hundred years would be very discouraging indeed. Nevertheless, Comenius' prediction actually had the opposite effect upon the Moravians. As a people devoted to self-sacrifice, they were honored to be able to help prepare the way for a future generation. This also enabled them to plan with a long-term strategy and vision that made possible some of their greatest contributions to the church and civilization.

Taking to heart his own prophecy about the continued one-hundred-year dormancy of the seed, Comenius planned to lay the strongest possible foundation for the future restoration he envisioned. He felt that the best way he could do this would be to dedicate his life entirely to the education of the young. One day, multiplied millions of the world's children would benefit from his plans.

WAR AND PEACE

Comenius believed that wars—which had brought so much tragedy to the world as well as to his own life—were the result of basic human ignorance. He dreamed of having schools for all children. This was a novel idea at the time since outside of a few Christian and Jewish communities, education was almost exclusively limited to the children of the nobility or the merchant class who were taught by private tutors.

Comenius was resolute in his belief that only a knowledge of the Prince of Peace could bring about peace among the nations. He viewed the Great Commission as a call to make *disciples*, or students. To him this was much more than just making converts. He believed that the Great Commission could never be fulfilled until schools founded on the gospel were established in every nation.

Comenius determined that in order to accomplish his goals he had to establish quality Christian schools. To do this he needed to provide excellent curriculum, materials and effective methods of teaching that not only imparted knowledge but also stimulated a *love* for knowledge. He set out to find teachers who possessed a deep love for God and were of strong moral character. He trained his teachers to impart both a love for God and a love of knowledge. With great passion, he devoted himself to seeing that each child would become "a creature which shall be the joy of his Creator."

In 1628 Comenius established a school in Lissa, Poland. Four years later he was made the bishop of the scattered Moravian brethren. Once his works were published, he quickly became widely known. One of his educational treatises, the *Janua Linguarum*, was even translated by the Moslems into Arabic, Turkish, Persian and Mongolian. His friends greatly rejoiced in this, believing that these translations would sow gospel seeds which would one day sprout into the Christian schools in all nations which he had envisioned.

CHRIST AS ALL

In 1641 Comenius was invited to England by Samuel Hartlib, a friend of the renowned poet Milton. There Comenius was persuaded to start his Pansophic College in London. His idea of pansophia was that the wisdom of God was sovereign over all things and all things were connected within the circle of this knowledge. He saw the Pansophic College as a place where Christian educators could gather together from Europe and America to seek a unity of knowledge through Christ in whom **"all things hold together"** (Colossians 1:17).

Comenius believed that education established on this basic knowledge of Christ as the reason for all things would bring unity to the Christian church. As Christians came into unity, they would then be able to spread the gospel to all nations, resulting in the unity of all nations and the end to war. It was this idea of taking the gospel to all nations that would fire the heart of the young Count Zinzendorf a century later and give birth to modern missions.

Although hopes were running high just before the college was to open, the English Civil War broke out, making it impossible to proceed. Comenius again refused to be discouraged, remarking that, "God has His own thoughts and seasons." He consoled himself with the fact that the Lord would not let David build His temple, but did allow him to prepare the design and materials for the next generation. Comenius determined to keep pursuing the vision and understanding that would one day be needed by the person God would choose to build the college.

WAR AND TRUTH

Comenius left for Sweden, where he had a major impact on the Swedish educational system through his relationship with the brilliant

Gustafsson Oxenstierna. In 1643 he returned to Lissa, Poland. He was then asked to come to America to serve as the first rector of the newly established Harvard University near Boston. He declined, deciding to stay in Lissa where he enjoyed a few peaceful years before war again struck a tragic blow to this great man of peace.

In 1656 the Catholic Poles defeated the Lutheran Swedes who occupied much of Poland. The Catholics condemned Lissa as a "heretic's nest" and it was burned. Again Comenius lost all his books and unpublished manuscripts.

Still refusing to be discouraged, Comenius became even more resolved that the truth of the gospel had to be made known. He knew that the only remedy for human folly was true education that led to the renewal of the mind by the true knowledge of Christ. He moved to the Netherlands where he spent the rest of his life.

In spite of the almost continuous tragedies and opposition Comenius faced, he published more than 90 books. His works on education helped to set the course of modern civilization. They gave new life to the church and propelled the modern democratic movements by empowering the common people with knowledge.

Comenius believed that the work of education was the special mandate of the church, which was called to be **"the light of the world" (Matthew 5:14)**. He interpreted light as being equivalent to knowledge, and he believed that true knowledge would always lead on to Christ Who was the Reason for all things.

Like his Savior and the great apostle Paul—and countless faithful believers since—Comenius died virtually alone, without being able to personally witness most of the fruit from his great labors. But he had faith, **"the assurance of things hoped for, the conviction of things not seen" (Hebrews 11:1)**. Like the heroes of the faith before him, he remained a stranger and exile on earth. He was a citizen of **"a better country" (Hebrews 11:16)** and never lost his vision for **"the city which has foundations, whose architect and builder is God" (Hebrews 11:10)**. For such people, God has prepared a city, because they **"endured, as seeing Him who is unseen" (Hebrews 11:27)**.

Through Tribulation He Entered the Kingdom

Satan had thought the best way to deal with Jesus was to crucify Him. Of course, that plan backfired to Satan's own destruction. In a similar way, he obviously thought that the best way to deal with Comenius was with wars, tragedies and the periodic destruction of his work. Even so, all that the enemy meant for evil was used to plant the seeds of an even greater vision in the heart of this great Moravian prophet.

These seeds would one day result in some of the greatest revivals in history. In turn, the seeds brought some of the greatest advancements in the human condition, which is always a fruit of true revival. The Lord loves all men and desires for them to be saved (I Timothy 2:4). He causes His sun to shine on the just and the unjust (Matthew 5:45). As Paul realized, **"the kindness of God leads you to repentance" (Romans 2:4).**

Those who trust their lives to the grace of God, regardless of persecutions or problems, are always used as the vessels of resurrection power. It is our hope in the resurrection that overcomes the enemy's greatest weapon against us—the fear of death. When the fear of death is conquered, all of his other yokes and devices are powerless. Those who live in the hope of the resurrection always prevail, and not only do they prevail, but they sow in the earth seeds that cannot die.

In II Kings 13:21 we have the remarkable story of a dead man who was cast into the grave of Elisha. Though the prophet was dead, there was still so much life in his bones that when the corpse touched those bones the man came back to life. The bones are but a person's "framework." The story of Elisha's bones illustrates that sometimes life will flow through us even when we just touch the framework of anointed vessels of God in history.

The hidden seed, first sown by John Hus and then kept alive by Comenius and Zinzendorf, is still alive. Many today who are touching just the framework of the ministries of these great men are being charged with resurrection power.

The following are a few of Comenius' other revolutionary ideas on education:

- He was one of the first to contend for the education of women and the children of all classes of people.

- He promoted a varied curriculum which included history, geography, science, music, singing, drama, civics and handiwork.

- He taught that everything in nature revealed Christ and that *true* science would always lead to a greater knowledge of the Creator.

- He believed that learning is facilitated by using all of our senses to interact with our environment, advocating a curriculum that employed seeing, touching, handling and smelling, rather than just hearing.

- He taught that the school environment was crucial and that classrooms should be bright and cheerful, reflecting the nature of truth.

- Since there were few pictures in books in the 17th century, he produced a children's encyclopedia with pictures called *Orbis Pictus*, believing that a picture could take the place of many words.

- According to Comenius, schools were to be "happy workshops of humanity" and "an imitation of heaven."

- He prescribed a considerable amount of play time in which he encouraged the teachers to participate.

- He taught that education was not just the acquisition of facts and knowledge, but the development of wisdom.

- He believed that school work should take no longer than four hours a day, leaving time for such things as amusement and domestic duties.

- He felt that homework was apt to be done poorly, and that poorly done work was more harmful than no work at all. He was also against homework because he felt the children's time at home could be better spent with their parents.

- He believed that children should learn by *doing* and by *teaching others*. Sometimes the older and more advanced children were required to instruct the younger.

- The children in his school were occasionally required to produce dramatic exhibitions related to what they were learning.

- He urged that education should be "in the spring of life and in the spring of day" (the morning).

- He advised, "let nothing be taught which is not of the most solid utility for this life or for the next."

- He understood the biblical principle of reproducing leaders, urging that each school should produce its own trained teachers by the apprenticeship system.

- He taught that as instruments of divine grace, teachers have a high calling. Yet he also sternly warned against professional arrogance saying, "Let your heavenly calling and the confidence of the parents who entrust their offspring to you be as a fire within you."

- The qualities he looked for in teachers included piety, diligence, paternal kindness, respect for children, the grace to accept frequent inspection, and the enthusiasm of "a miner who trembles with excitement when he discovers a rich vein of ore."

THE REBIRTH OF THE REFORMATION

By the early 1700s, the momentum of the Reformation had diminished from an avalanche to a few pebbles rolling down the hill. The Lutheran movement that had so impacted the world made the most fatal mistake a movement can make—it stopped *moving*! Once the movement ceased to grow in vision, the process of territorial preservation began.

The work of the Protestant reformers crystallized into increasingly divided institutions that displayed many of the same characteristics as the oppressive church they had so valiantly fought. Soon they too were persecuting those who dared to go beyond their own narrowly defined parameters of spiritual truth. After accomplishing so much for truth and freedom, the Reformation movements themselves became resisters of both truth and freedom.

History testifies that when the church loses the dynamic of growth and change, she loses both her impact on the world and her relevancy to her own people. From Paul's metaphorical comparison of the Word of God to water (Ephesians 5:26), we can see that, like water, the truth of the Word must keep flowing in order to stay pure. By 1700 the Reformation had been reduced from a mighty river of life dramatically changing the spiritual landscape of the world, to a dam trying to contain and hold back the waters. Because of this, the waters were fast becoming stagnant and lifeless.

This tendency on the part of the institutional church, whether Catholic or Protestant, gave birth to what are today considered "renewal" ministries. These usually did not intend to start new churches, but set out simply to renew the existing church. Like the "reformers" before them, those with a vision of renewal never meant to begin new churches or movements; they only wanted to restore the spiritual purity of the existing church. Even so, almost every true prophetic voice was used not only to renew the existing church but also to start movements and new churches that would bring about a further advancement of the kingdom. However, by 1700 the Reformation churches were themselves in need of both renewal and further reformation.

THE PICTURE BELOW IS OF RICK JOYNER, JOHN DAWSON AND LEONARD JONES STANDING BY THE GRAVE OF JON AMOS COMENIUS NEAR AMSTERDAM, THE NETHERLANDS.

THE THIRD WITNESS:

COUNT NIKOLAUS LUDWIG VON ZINZENDORF (1700-1760)

May 26, 1700 brought the timely birth of Count Nikolaus Ludwig von Zinzendorf to the German Count George Ludwig and Baroness Charlotte Zinzendorf. This young count would be used to spark another spiritual revolution, one that was profoundly different from those preceding it.

Historians have called Count Zinzendorf "the rich young ruler who said 'yes.'" Born into one of the great families of Europe and destined to sit on the court of one of the continent's most powerful thrones, he gave it all up and spent his life and fortune to carry the gospel to the ends of the earth. This one man's zeal for the Lord so transformed modern Christianity that it would be impossible to measure the full impact of his life on the church or the world. He gave birth to modern missions, renewed the Moravian church, and illuminated the great Reformation truths so that they became a practical lifestyle for every home. Zinzendorf set an example of integrity in ministry that would be a standard for generations.

The story of Zinzendorf is one of history's greatest examples of how a pure love for the Lord can propel a man to a spiritual power that not only impacts his own time, but places his mark dramatically on every century that follows. The Moravians were reborn as a movement through the ministry of Zinzendorf, and their rebirth had widespread repercussions. Although the Moravians may not have been the main *body* of the Reformation, they were in many ways the *spirit*—hidden and mysterious, but the true essence of power.

Zinzendorf did not set out to change anyone's mind or doctrines. He loved Catholics as much as he loved Lutherans, and he remained a Lutheran until his death. Zinzendorf, like a handful of great souls before him, touched something so sublime and noble that true believers of every doctrinal persuasion wanted to claim him as their own, even though many of their own doctrinal prejudices were being shattered by the influence of his life.

The power of Zinzendorf's life was his passionate love for Jesus. His love for the Lord exuded with such a noble spirit that it made the disputes and arguments of the erudite theological schools of his day seem profane and irrelevant by comparison. If Luther had changed the church by standing for truth, Zinzendorf changed it by standing for love. This love brought the Reformation to a new level. The change he brought did not come from further ecclesiastical introspection but by looking outwardly at a needy world.

Up to that time, the Reformation had been fueled almost exclusively by a commitment to doctrinal truth. Although this helped to lay a solid foundation for the progress that was to come, it also brought with it a great danger, for **"the letter kills, but the Spirit gives life" (II Corinthians 3:6).**

Vast numbers of people were killed on battlefields because of conflicts over Reformation truths—perhaps even more people than had been saved by those truths. Zinzendorf helped to change the focus of the advancing church from *what* they believed to *how* they believed. He did not just *believe* the great Christian truths, he *lived* them. He was not the first to do this, but he did it with such strength of character that the world was forced to take notice.

A New Stream in the River of Life

During the century preceeding Zinzendorf's birth, a new movement called "Pietism" had begun to flow through the church. Prior to this, the Reformation had emphasized the renewal of the *institution* of the church. This new movement, however, was basically devoted to the spiritual rebirth and renewal of *individuals*.

Pietism took the biblical truths recovered by Reformation leaders and applied them to life. In essence, they declared that it was not enough for a person to intellectually know that **"the just shall live by faith" (Romans 1:17 KJV)**. Instead, the pietists urged that we as individuals must actually *have faith*. Pietism emphasized that mere intellectual assent to doctrines accomplished little if they were not reflected in our lifestyle and accompanied by the fruit of the Spirit.

To present-day evangelicals, these truths may seem obvious, but at the time they stirred a radical and controversial movement that impacted the Reformation churches as much as the Reformation churches had impacted Catholicism. Pietism brought down the wrath of the theological authorities, and it is still often maligned by theological schools today.

When Luther's revelation that **"the just shall live by faith" (Romans 1:17)** is applied *doctrinally* but not *experientially*, the result is that mere agreement with a doctrine makes one a Lutheran rather than a personal experience, a personal revelation of truth, or a life that reflects the truth. This "personal faith" was considered an affront to the state religion, and it continues to be an affront to all who seek to institutionalize faith in God.

There were many extreme elements which emerged from the Pietist Movement or tried to align themselves with it. Even so, it is a fundamental deception to judge any theology, church or movement by its most extreme elements. Both the Pietists and the established Reformation camps were guilty of doing this to each other, leading to considerable and unnecessary divisions. Yet both camps ultimately had an important and beneficial impact on the other.

It could be argued that without the Pietists' infusion of devotion to intimacy with Christ, the Reformation would have died from self-inflicted wounds. It can also be argued that without the infusion of the disciplines from mainline Reformers, the Pietists would have drifted into spiritual anarchy and irrelevancy.

Both the new and the old almost certainly would have died if they had not found their essential relationship with each other. Zinzendorf was possibly the most important bridge-builder between the two.

A NEW VISION OF UNITY

Zinzendorf is believed to be the first churchman to actually use the term "ecumenism." He believed the Scriptures taught that there was only one church, and that all true believers—whether Lutherans, Moravians or Catholics—were brothers in Christ. This was a message far ahead of its time and caused considerable controversy.

However, Zinzendorf's conviction about the unity of the church was the result of an even more radical comprehension of truth: that faith in God is personal and substantive, not just institutional or doctrinal. Because Zinzendorf recognized true faith as personal, he was free to have fellowship with anyone who knew and loved the Savior, regardless of their institutional affiliation. The Count never attacked or tried to undermine institutions—he simply rose above them. He sought to know men after the Spirit rather than by externals, such as doctrinal or institutional affiliation.

Zinzendorf not only *taught* about unity, he *lived* it. He loved and befriended Lutherans, Moravians, Pietists, Puritans, Anabaptists and Catholics who truly loved the Savior. To this day, many from various doctrinal persuasions have appreciated the history of Zinzendorf and have been impacted by the power of his witness. The influence of such a great soul could not be contained in a single institution.

FORTIFIED IN HIS WORD

After his birth, Zinzendorf's mother implored the Lord to "govern the heart of this child that he may walk blamelessly in the path of virtue...that his path may be fortified in His Word." This prayer was answered quickly, for the young Count developed a deep passion for the Scriptures. He esteemed the Word of God as more precious than his great riches. Throughout his life, Zinzendorf spent almost all of his free time searching and pondering Scripture. This zeal for the Bible not only helped to direct his own life, but it affected many other future leaders of the church.

From a very young age, Zinzendorf seemed able to distinguish between those who had true spiritual authority and those who just occupied official positions in the church. He was raised in an atmosphere of prayer, worship and study of the Bible under the care of Lady Gersdorf and his Aunt Henrietta. Zinzendorf's recognition of the authority of God in the faithful Henrietta and Lady Gersdorf made him sensitive to the true life of Christ in any person, regardless of their ecclesiastical or political positions. This later enabled him to draw out of carpenters and common laborers the light of Christ that would ultimately touch nations.

Like the faithful women in the gospels, these ladies followed Jesus. The presence of the Lord emanated from them, and their love for Him was contagious. The young Zinzendorf became so infected with their passion that he also was addicted to the Lord's presence his entire life.

Even as a young child, Zinzendorf wrote love letters to Jesus and impacted others by his spiritual passion. John Weinlick wrote in his book, *Count Zinzendorf*, "When Swedish soldiers captured the castle in which the six-year-old Count was staying, they burst into his room while he was having his devotions. They were awed as they heard the boy speak and pray." The incident was a prophetic indication of the way the Count would move many others with the depth of his personal communion with the Lord throughout the rest of his sixty years.

A CONFLICT OF CALLING

The Count, who was so destined to champion personal faith and relationship to God, was not allowed to easily forget his earthly birthright—sitting on one of the highest imperial courts. Zinzendorf was tutored and disciplined in the necessary culture for his expected service to the court. At age ten he was sent by his guardian, Count Otto Christian, to be discipled under the strict pietist, August Francke. By age 15, he could read the classics and the Greek New Testament, and in addition to his native German, was fluent in Latin and French. During this time, Zinzendorf began to display an extraordinary poetic gift which one biographer said enabled him to compose hymns even faster than his thoughts could be put on paper.

While staying in the home of Francke, the young count was exposed to two evangelists who had been sent to India by the Danish-Halle mission. At meals and daily meetings, these men recounted their experiences preaching the gospel in foreign lands. To young Zinzendorf, these stories sounded like a modern Book of Acts. He was stirred with a passion for preaching the gospel. Zinzendorf would spend the rest of his life growing in two great passions: getting closer to Jesus and sharing Him with those who had never heard the gospel.

The Count continued his university studies at Wittenberg. This was the seedbed of the Reformation and the fortress of Lutheran orthodoxy, which was not friendly toward Pietism. His guardian prescribed a strict schedule from seven in the morning until ten at night in the study of civil law, the history of the German states and other subjects deemed necessary for his future place on the Emperor's court. Even so, Zinzendorf still found more than two hours a day for prayer and the study of the Scriptures. Each day the dichotomy of these two callings waged war for both his soul and, as we can see in retrospect, the future of the church.

THE GRACE OF TOLERANCE

In spite of the university leadership's opposition to Pietism which the Count embraced,

Zinzendorf learned to appreciate their position and learn from it. He always seemed able to find and draw out the best in men while overlooking their faults. This characteristic would enable him to rise above the petty spiritual politics that thwart so many in their quest for truth.

Because of this spiritual magnanimity, the Count was able to touch the essence of spiritual truth—truth that sets men free to transcend the temporary realm of institutions and live in the eternal realm of the kingdom of God. We will always have critics with us, but they are never remembered past their own time. True spiritual sojourners like Zinzendorf plant their influence in every succeeding generation because they live in an eternity which cannot pass away.

After completing his studies at Wittenberg, Zinzendorf began a tour of the great learning centers of Europe. While in Paris, he met and formed a strong bond with the Roman Catholic Cardinal Noailles, a man of deep faith and rich spiritual vision. Even though this relationship would cause considerable controversy for Zinzendorf over the years, the Count remained committed to never judging a man by his doctrinal or denominational affiliation, but only by the content of his heart.

This grace, maintained by the Count so uncompromisingly throughout his life, ultimately impacted the churches in both Europe and America. His demonstration of a higher vision—the ability to know others by the Spirit and not just according to externals—raised the level of grace and spirituality of the entire church. It laid the groundwork for men such as George Whitfield, who was a staunch Calvinist, and John Wesley, a committed Armenian, to so love and esteem each other that they could combine their spiritual firepower to ignite history-changing revivals.

While completing his tour of the great European cities, the Count visited an art museum in Dusseldorf. There he encountered Domencio Feti's *Ecce Homo* ("Behold the Man"), a striking portrait of Jesus crowned with thorns. The inscription read, "I have done this for you. What have you done for Me?" Zinzendorf was stunned. "I have loved him for so long," mused the young nobleman, "but I have not really done anything for Him."

Standing before the portrait, the Count made a commitment that became the compelling focus of the rest of his life. "From now on, I will do whatever He leads me to do," he vowed. Zinzendorf stayed true to this commitment, continually seeking to know the Lord's will and devoting himself with unrelenting resolve to accomplish it. That day, a rich young ruler said "yes" to the call of Christ, and the world he forsook would be changed because of it.

THE THREE CORDS OF VISION

From the day of the Count's commitment, three dynamic foundational forces were combined in his life. Together they provided a force powerful enough to turn the great ship of human history a few significant degrees:

- **Passion** for the Savior kept Zinzendorf's faith from being passive. Passion transforms emotions into actions.

- **Prophetic Vision** enabled Zinzendorf to see and embrace truth wherever, or in whomever, it was found. This allowed the Count to cross barriers to truth that often blocked other men.

- **Purpose** awakened Zinzendorf to the fact that there was no higher calling in this life than to serve the Lord. It was this clarity of *purpose* that combined his *passion* and *prophetic vision* into a living force called FAITH. This faith would move mountains and build highways in their place.

Many who have passion for the Lord and accomplish exploits for Him are limited by the narrowness of their vision. Others have passion and vision, but are limited because they do not combine them with a well-planned strategy. Zinzendorf was able to focus his passion and vision into a *mission*—sharing the love of the Savior with those who had never had the opportunity to hear of Him. This "mission" became known as "missions," and those who shared it became known as "missionaries."

It could be argued that the religious refugees from Moravia, who were personally touched by this powerful new mission of Zinzendorf's, became the most spiritual, noble, self-sacrifice body of believers since the first-century church. It could also be argued that the world has probably not witnessed a movement of this quality since.

Like every other significant movement in church history, the Moravians were not without their faults and failures, but they were not stopped by them. They may have stumbled, fallen and run into obstacles, but they always got right back up and refused to stop running until they finished their course. This is the ultimate test—true love will never quit. Many have started the race and run well for a period of time, but few have been able to run until they finished their course. Only those with true love and true faith are able to keep going despite seemingly insurmountable obstacles.

The highborn young Count, raised to be the confidante of kings, could have sat in the highest positions on the court of one of the great thrones of Europe. Yet he began to dream more about becoming a pastor than being in politics. However, when he shared his desire to be ordained, he was rebuked by churchmen as well as the nobility. Even so, the Count was resolute, viewing the pastorate as a higher calling than the court.

Zinzendorf turned from the studies meant to prepare him for the court and began to study for the ministry. This was a great battle for him. There were times when he would give in and serve on the court, but he was never at peace until he gave himself fully to the ministry of the Word and prayer. This rich young ruler really had said "yes" to the Lord, and he was willing to sacrifice everything to obey Him.

A MARRIAGE MADE IN HEAVEN

In his position, it was proper for the Count to choose a wife whose connections would serve him politically and financially. Instead, Zinzendorf chose a bride who could help him *spiritually*, marrying the Countess Erdmuth Dorethea von Reuss. It was said by some that her home was even more devoted to Pietism than his own.

Zinzendorf's biographer Weinlick wrote, "Romantic love had a minor place in the courtship, and set a pattern for the kind of marriage soon to become common in the renewed Moravian Church." Every choice was viewed from its spiritual potential rather than its temporal importance. The interests of the Savior were esteemed above personal interests.

The young Countess proved to be more than just an encouragement and help to the Count. Because of her considerable contribution to the movement, she became known as "the mother of the Moravian church." She committed herself to "a life of self-denial...to assist in gaining souls for Christ." She lived this commitment to such a degree that it seems unlikely the impending spiritual advance, one of the greatest in church history, could have been possible without her.

She loved the Count and their twelve children, but she always kept the interests of the kingdom of God first. The Countess not only freed her husband to embark on long missionary journeys (some to North America lasted for years), but she also showed great wisdom in practical matters, proving herself to be a capable manager in finances and the upkeep of the estates. She did everything possible to free the Count to give himself fully to the ministry. In the midst of all of these duties, this remarkable woman also found time to make extensive travels on the continent and in England, witnessing boldly for the Lord and encouraging the dispersed Pietist societies to be resolute in the faith.

Immediately after their marriage, the young couple moved to Dresden. There the Count tried to occupy himself with the matters of state, but they were so boring to him compared to the matters of the kingdom that he resolved to give himself fully to the ministry. At that opportune time, a lone Christian refugee from Moravia showed up at his door. This refugee's name was Christian

David and he had heard that the Pietist Zinzendorf might allow the oppressed Moravian refugees a haven on his land. The Count was more than just *willing* to help them—he was *eager*.

THE "MORAVIAN MOSES"

Christian David is credited by historians as being one of the two individuals most responsible for the spiritual birth of the Christian community at Herrnhut. This was the name of Zinzendorf's estate and meant "under the Lord's watch." A humble carpenter, David was brought up as a Catholic but could find no spiritual satisfaction there. At age 20, David obtained a German Bible and began his quest for truth. This resulted in a profound conversion.

In 1719 he married and began making personal evangelistic trips into Moravia. There he happened upon the Brethren who longed for the rebirth of a true New Testament church and were holding tenaciously to the prophetic word of John Hus that such a church would yet live. After David met Count Zinzendorf, he returned to Moravia for the oppressed but devoted saints and led them to the Zinzendorf estate. David then began the settlement by felling the first tree as he recited Psalm 84:

How lovely are Thy dwelling places,
O Lord of hosts!

My soul longed and even yearned for
the courts of the Lord;
My heart and my flesh sing for joy to
the living God.

The bird also has found a house,
And the swallow a nest for herself,
where she may lay her young,
Even Thine altars, O Lord of hosts,
My King and my God.

How blessed are those who dwell in Thy
house!
They are ever praising Thee.

How blessed is the man whose strength
is in Thee;
In whose heart are the highways to Zion!

Passing through the valley of Baca, they
make it a spring,
The early rain also covers it with blessings.

They go from strength to strength,
Every one of them appears before God
in Zion.

O Lord God of hosts, hear my prayer;
Give ear, O God of Jacob!

Behold our shield, O God,
And look upon the face of Thine anointed.

For a day in Thy courts is better than a
thousand outside.
I would rather stand at the threshold of
the house of my God,
Than dwell in the tents of wickedness.

For the Lord God is a sun and shield;
The Lord gives grace and glory;
No good thing does He withhold from
those who walk uprightly.

O Lord of hosts,
How blessed is the man who trusts in Thee!

David crossed the border ten times and led
the faithful to freedom, for which Zinzendorf
dubbed him "the Moravian Moses." David was
prone to poor judgment and was at times
carried away by false teachers or rebellious
faultfinders. But he always repented and
returned to the simplicity of devotion to Christ
and the vision of Herrnhut.

SEEKING A "HEAVENLY CITY"

Not until the Christmas of 1722 did Zinzendorf pay much attention to the six adults and
four children who occupied the first new
dwelling on his estate. One day as he and the
Countess passed the cottage, they stopped to
pray with them. Zinzendorf at once felt a
spiritual kinship. With this fellowship, his
vision of a Christian community began. From
that time on, Zinzendorf's zeal would spread

primarily through the *"Unitas Fratrum"* (United Brethren), which was the popular name for the Moravian Church. With Zinzendorf's encouragement and participation, the leaders of "the hidden seed" began to believe their spiritual exile was over.

By 1725 the Zinzendorf estate had become a small city. Sympathetic Catholics heroically aided the escape of many believers from Moravia, blessing them on the journey to their promised land at Herrnhut. Not only did Moravians join the new community of believers, but also Lutheran Pietists, former Catholics, Separatists, Reformed and Anabaptists. They were all seeking the fellowship of others who were looking for a heavenly city **"whose architect and builder is God" (Hebrews 11:10).**

For a short period, Herrnhut would become possibly the closest example of that heavenly city to be found on the earth. However, the community would not attain such spiritual heights without overcoming the obstacles that had thwarted multitudes of others before them. They sought to establish a genuine spiritual unity among those of different doctrinal persuasions, while facing the multitude of personality conflicts that arise any time people truly begin to grow close.

As could be expected, trouble arose quickly in the young community. By 1726 a sharp disagreement had arisen between the Lutherans and the Moravians over the liturgy of the Sunday service. This was just the most visible of many other disputes that arose over doctrine, language, and the economic pressures of supporting the community that had swelled to more than 300. Every group was seeking to impose its own agenda on the entire community, and each agenda created further division.

Just as the strains were becoming critical, a false teacher took up residence in the community. This man brought with him bitterness toward the Lutherans who had expelled him, and his root of bitterness quickly began to defile many, just as Hebrews 12:15 warns will happen. Taking a great personal dislike for Zinzendorf, he began to preach that the Count was none other than "the beast" mentioned in the Book of Revelation. Even Christian David was carried away with his preposterous doctrine for a time.

A Shepherd's Heart

When it appeared that the community was going to come apart at the seams, Zinzendorf decided to move from Dresden and set up residence in the academy building on the estate. With a true pastor's heart, the Count began going from house to house, counseling each family from the Scriptures. It took time and patience, but eventually love and a spirit of cooperation began to prevail. In May of 1727, the Count established a set of manorial rules for Herrnhut. By then the community was ready to embrace them with a "Brotherly Agreement" between each other and the Lord.

Next, twelve responsible men were elected elders. Night watchmen were appointed, as well as watchers for the sick and aides to distribute goods to the poor. Then Zinzendorf, who has been called "a genius for quickening and giving expression to Christian fellowship," instituted "bands" of small groups of believers who had "a special spiritual affinity" to each other.

These "bands" began to meet together in homes for the purpose of encouraging one another in the faith. These had such a powerful impact on the spiritual maturity of the community that the Count later stated that "without them the Brethren's Church would never have become what it is." Each of these bands had an appointed leader, and every brother and sister in the community became a part of one. This was possibly the beginning of modern home fellowship groups, which provided such a strong foundation for Wesley's revivals and many others that followed.

Zinzendorf's wise and decisive leadership was quickly paying dividends, and it seemed almost weekly that the spiritual unity and the bonds of love were becoming perceptively stronger. The night watchers announced the hours with a hymn, and the small groups began holding all-night prayer vigils. The young Count was teaching and exhorting daily, moving from group to group and house to house. The physical community was becoming a *heart* community as more and more homes were opening day and night for prayer, fellowship and teaching.

In July, as Zinzendorf was browsing in a library in Zitau, he happened upon a copy of the constitution of the *Unitas Fratrum,* written by none other than Jon Amos Comenius. The amazed Count quickly understood the importance of this discovery—that the Moravian

Brethren were "a fully established church antedating Lutheranism itself." He was also astonished by the similarities between this constitution and the recently adopted "Brotherly Agreement."

The Count was profoundly impacted by this discovery, which so clearly confirmed the divine destiny resting upon the humble refugees to whom he had opened his estate. He quickly translated portions of the constitution of the *Unitas Fratrum* into German and returned to Herrnhut to share them with the Moravians.

As Zinzendorf poured over the writings of Comenius, he was amazed by how accurately they articulated some of the deepest burdens of his own heart. Then he came upon the prophecy of Comenius that the hidden seed would sprout in one hundred years. When he realized that his discovery of Comenius' writings took place a hundred years after the prophecy, almost to the day, a new resolve was ignited within him. This new sense of destiny for the Count and the Moravian refugees resulted in the meeting that is now recorded in history as the "Moravian Pentecost."

The Moravian community was established at Herrnhut in 1722, and the "Moravian

Pentecost" occurred five years later. After one hundred years, the seed had sprung to life as one of the great Christian movements of all time. They called themselves *"The Unitus Fratrum,"* or "The Unity of the Brethren," but are still affectionately known throughout the church and the world as "The Moravians."

Since the days of the apostles Peter, Paul and John, it is possible that no other three men within the same movement have so impacted the church and the world as Jon Hus, Jon Amos Comenius, and Count Nikolaus Ludwig von Zinzendorf. One planted the seed, one watered it, and one reaped the fruit (see I Corinthians 3:6).

A FOUNDATION FOR VISITATION

When we walk by the light of true vision, unity is inevitable. **"If we walk in the light as He Himself is in the light,** *we have fellowship with one another"* **(I John 1:7).** True spiritual fellowship is the result of vision—seeing the light. Darkness separated us from God and each other, but true light reunites us. As vision increased at Herrnhut, unity likewise increased. This has been the formula for every visitation of God since Pentecost.

True spiritual vision is built upon a solid historical foundation. We must recognize our past to accurately know our future. When Jesus was asked by what authority He did His works, He replied by asking His inquisitors whether the baptism of John was of God or from men (Matthew 21:23-27). John the Baptist was the last of the old order and was sent to verify the One of whom the prophets of old had all spoken—the One who would bring the new order.

Jesus did not belittle John as a member of "the old order," but rather honored him and submitted to his baptism. This not only acknowledged John's authority, but also honored all those who had prepared the way before Jesus came. Jesus actually pointed to John's baptism as verification of His *own* authority. This points to a "continuation principle" that is a prerequisite for true spiritual authority.

It is important for us to be in unity with the contemporary church, but it is also essential that we be in unity with the historic church. None of us would be able to advance the purposes of the kingdom if those who have gone before us had not already made the highway to our present point. Because **"God** is opposed to the proud, but gives grace to the humble" (James 4:6), many fail to fully walk in their own calling because their arrogance toward previous spiritual generations causes them to stumble.

The race that we have been called to run is a "relay race." It does not matter whether we run the first leg or the last, since it is the *whole team* that will be credited with the victory. If we pridefully consider those who have gone before us as inferior, we have not only cut ourselves off from our past, but we have also broken the "relay" that connects us with our future. As the Lord established in the Ten Commandments (Exodus 20:12), long life comes from honoring our fathers and mothers—and this principle applies to honoring our *spiritual* fathers and mothers as well as our natural ones.

When the Count discovered the constitution of the *Unitas Fratrum*, he was able to clearly see the destiny of the Moravians because he recognized their historic foundation. This solidified the people of Herrnhut into a prayerful, united community with faith in their calling and purpose. Not only were they growing in unity with each other, but the Count's discovery at Zitau made them now feel a genuine link and sense of unity with the saints who had gone before them. As they recognized the hand of God in their history, their future steps were clearly outlined for them. This powerful sense of purpose propelled them into the future with the great boldness required by their destiny.

When men recognize their common destiny, divisive personal agendas and petty doctrinal differences fade into insignificance. Then the true unity of the Spirit becomes possible. The unity of the Spirit requires, first of all, the *presence* of the Holy Spirit. To maintain the Spirit's presence, we must **"not grieve the Holy Spirit of God,"** as Paul exhorted the Ephesians (Ephesians 4:30). Paul continued by giving instructions on *how* to avoid grieving the Spirit: **"Let all bitterness and wrath and anger and clamor and slander be put away from you, along with all malice. And be kind to one another, tender-hearted, forgiving each other, just as God in Christ also has forgiven you"** (4:31-32).

Church history began when the Holy Spirit descended upon the praying believers who had gathered in **"one accord"** at Pentecost (see Acts 2:1-4 KJV). Church history testifies that almost every revival or visitation of God is preceded by believers coming into unity. As the community at Herrnhut moved into increasing unity during the summer of 1727, an expectation of something wonderful began to permeate the Zinzendorf estate. The settlement *Diary* recorded that, "There was evidence of the fire of love."

Christian David recommended that a study be made of the Epistles of John. On August 5, Zinzendorf and a group of the brethren spent the entire night in prayer and sharing the wonders of the Lord. Anticipation was building to the point where many did not want to sleep for fear that they would miss something God was doing.

THE MORAVIAN PENTECOST

On Wednesday, August 13, 1727, at the first communion service of the reconciled community, the Holy Spirit fell upon the gathered believers with such power that historians call it "the Moravian Pentecost." The day began with a message on the Lord's supper by one of the believers named Rothe. As the people walked the mile from the settlement to the church at Berthelsdorf for the service, it seemed as though they were all enveloped in a special cloud of love and mutual admiration.

Through the experiences of the preceding weeks, all the exiles had been humbled under an intense conviction of their sin and spiritual helplessness, causing them to begin esteeming others more highly than themselves. The mutual kindness and affection were even more striking considering the great conflict the settlement had just weathered. The spirit of conviction that had come upon the Moravians and the deepening humility and love that followed seemed to touch the very heart of the Holy Spirit in such a way that He could not resist pouring out His power on them.

As Rothe pronounced a "truly apostolic blessing" upon two young girls who were being confirmed, the congregation knelt and sang: *My soul before Thee prostrate lies, to Thee its source, my spirit flies.* Then prayers of great unction rose from the brethren as they interceded for each other and those who were still living under the persecution in Moravia.

The Holy Spirit swept across them in waves as the passion of the Lamb of God gripped their hearts. The awesome benefits of His sacrifice became so real to them that for years to come this little band proved willing to sacrifice everything for Him. In the testimony of one Moravian: "We discovered therein the finger of God, and found ourselves, as it were, baptized under the cloud of our fathers, with their spirit. For that Spirit came again upon us, and great signs and wonders were wrought among the Brethren in those days, and *great grace* prevailed among us, and in the whole country."

The outpouring of the Holy Spirit at Herrnhut did not result in spiritual arrogance among those who received it, but rather the opposite. It branded the cross upon their hearts to such an extent that they could no longer bear to go on living just for themselves, but instead were compelled to **"do all things for the sake of the gospel" (I Corinthians 9:23).** Constant sacrifice and the laying down of their own self-interest became as much a part of Herrnhut as their daily meals.

The spirit of sacrifice kindled at the Moravian Pentecost released the power for a humble group of exiles, led by an unlikely nobleman, to change the course of Christianity and impact the history of the world. **"The cross...is the power of God" (I Corinthians 1:18),** and individuals who embrace the cross will know the power of God in their lives.

When the cross is embraced by an entire church or community such as Herrnhut, God's power will be witnessed by the world.

THE BIRTH OF MODERN MISSIONS

The immediate result of the outpouring of the Spirit at the first Pentecost in Jerusalem was the conversion of those who were gathered **"from every nation under heaven" (Acts 2:5).** The first result of the Moravian Pentecost was, in a similar way, the compulsion to go to every nation under heaven with the gospel. **"God so loved the world, that He gave His only begotten Son" (John 3:16).** It seems that all who truly receive the Son are touched by God's love for the world—and they are compelled to go to the world with that message.

When Peter received the revelation from the Father that Jesus was the Christ and was filled with the Holy Spirit at Pentecost, it was inevitable that he would be moved to tell others that the church age would be born and thousands would come into the kingdom. It is not believing in our minds, but in our hearts, that results in righteousness (Romans 10:10). Those who have the truth revealed in their hearts have a power to speak truth that includes more than an ability to touch people's minds—they can move people's *hearts*.

The rock upon which the Lord would build His church again in the days of the Moravians was the same revelation that Peter received from the Father (Matthew 16:15-19). The church would not be built by brilliant minds, but by burning hearts. The Moravian Pentecost was a revelation from the Father of the centrality and power of the cross and the love of God that is manifested by the cross.

The cross would never again be a mere symbol or intellectual concept to them. It was a passion that burned with such intensity that some in this community actually sold themselves as slaves so that they could reach the slaves. Others built missionary outposts that would result in a martyr for each soul saved, yet they never lacked volunteers.

Leo Tolstoy once said, "True prophecy is like a fire that is lit in a dry wood—it will burn and burn until all of the wood, hay and stubble is consumed." The Bible makes it clear: **"The testimony of Jesus is the spirit of prophecy" (Revelation 19:10)**, and **"our God is a consuming fire" (Hebrews 12:29)**. The Lord instituted the church to be His dwelling place, and Jesus' home is in the hearts of His people. Therefore, His people should always be on fire.

Many spiritual movements have been sparked by the rediscovery and presentation of certain biblical truths, and these movements have done some good. But when a movement is begun with a foundation of the centrality of Christ and a love for Him, a fire begins to burn that cannot be put out. It will burn until the wood, hay and stubble are consumed, while the gold, silver and precious stones of truth are purified.

The fire that was ignited in the little Moravian community at Herrnhut spread until it had set both England and America ablaze with the First Great Awakening. It is possible that every subsequent awakening could be traced to the principles that were first instituted at Herrnhut.

THE SEEDS WILL SPROUT AGAIN

It would be a serious delusion to look at the church today and claim that she has attained **"the unity of the faith...the knowledge of the Son of God, to a mature man, to the measure of the stature which belongs to the fullness of Christ" (Ephesians 4:13).** The reformation of the church has not yet been completed.

Each reform movement began with the recovery of biblical truths that were lost or diminished during the Middle Ages. Every true movement since the First Great Awakening has been characterized by the centrality of the cross, a conviction of sin, a renewed passion for the Son of God, and the need for believers to take up their own crosses and live lives of sacrifice. This all results in the noble purpose of spreading the gospel of Jesus Christ.

Many get distracted from the River of Life by the tributaries that feed it, allowing individual truths to divert them from following the Truth Himself. Few have ever navigated the River of Life without ever being distracted, and the Moravians themselves were at times caught in side eddies that waylaid their journey. Even so, they always found their way back to midstream and focused again on loving the Son of God. The love of Jesus is the compass that keeps us heading toward the City of God.

It could be said that since the Reformation began, Zinzendorf and the Moravians have best navigated the River that brings renewal to the church, leaving us with one of the most accurate maps to follow. Many great leaders of subsequent spiritual advances have pointed back to the Moravians as a source of their inspiration.

THE LIFE OF THE COMMUNITY

For five years after the Moravian Pentecost, the community at Herrnhut was captivated by seeking to behold the glory of the Son of God. Their community so reflected the atmosphere of heaven that John Wesley would one day call it "the place on earth that is possibly the most like the New Jerusalem in heaven." The extraordinary life found in this community flourished because community was not what they were looking for. Many who have tried to follow in their steps have made community life itself the ideal, and even the idol. But the Moravians managed to avoid this pitfall. They had community because they were seeking *Christ* instead of seeking *community*.

As long as the exiles kept their attention on Jesus, the glory prevailed. Whenever they would start to look at each other, or even begin to focus too much on their work for Him, the glory would depart. Even missions could not be allowed to eclipse Christ as the center, or they would begin to lose the fuel that kept the fire going.

King David wrote, **"Behold, how good and how pleasant it is for brothers to dwell together in unity!" (Psalm 133:1)** Christians in every generation of church history have yearned for the type of community of believers described in the Book of Acts. Men were created to worship God while in fellowship with one another. Since the fall, men have had a void in their hearts that can only be filled by a reunion with God. Since the Tower of Babel, they have had a void that can only be filled by a reunion with their fellow men. True Christian community, which is true church life, fills the deepest yearnings of the human heart—yearnings that can be filled by nothing else.

For a period of time, Herrnhut may have been the greatest example of Christian fellowship since the first-century church. Their worship gave birth to some of the greatest hymns ever produced, which are still used around the world. Their devotion to prayer led to one hundred years of continuous, around-the-clock intercession that has been an inspiration and standard for possibly every prayer movement since.

The Moravians' love for the lost compelled them to send missionaries to the ends of the earth. This was truly the birth of the modern missionary movement, for which they are still one of the greatest inspirations and examples. Herrnhut was such a light in its time that John Wesley not only said it might be the closest thing to the New Jerusalem that could be found on the earth, but he added, "I would gladly have spent my life there."

Since the days of Herrnhut, many have unsuccessfully tried to duplicate the essence and spiritual fire of this community. Wherever true zeal for the Lord emerges, it seems inevitable that at least some are stirred with a vision of community. However, this seemingly noble objective is where many have been diverted from the path. As stated, the success of Herrnhut as a community was the result of having a higher vision than community. To them, community was merely a means, not an end in itself. Like anything else, whenever community itself becomes the vision, it inevitably becomes an idol that eclipses the worship of Christ.

Nevertheless, it appears almost inevitable that those who are moving toward higher worship and devotion to Christ will also move toward community—or "common-unity"—with one another. To the idealist, this often means having all things in common, as was the case in the first-century Jerusalem church. But this was not the case at Herrnhut, and seldom has it been the case in any truly successful Christian community.

There is something higher than having all our possessions as common property with each other: it is truly giving everything to the Lord and learning to be faithful stewards. This is not to negate the possibility that there will be times when having all things in common may be necessary—but it should be the exception rather than the rule.

A community like Herrnhut, where there is such pure worship and devotion to missions, may be one of the ultimate expressions of Christianity. Yet when this is attempted prematurely out of spiritual idealism, the results are usually tragic. At Herrnhut, as in first-century Jerusalem, community was the by-product of a much higher vision, and that is almost certainly the only way true Christian community will ever exist.

REVIVAL AND REVOLUTION

The church of the early eighteenth century was almost as much a political entity as it was spiritual. With few exceptions, a nation was either Protestant or Catholic because of battles that had been fought for control, not because of a true spiritual movement or revival. Instead of being "born again" into the kingdom of God (John 3:3), a person was typically born into the state church that was recognized by the nation they inhabited.

At that time, there was little or no emphasis on having a personal conversion or relationship to God. Faith was demonstrated by acceptance of the creeds of the state church. To send missionaries from a state church to another nation would have had serious political consequences, since it was considered the equivalent of an invasion.

Because the emphasis of Christianity during that period was on the state and the institution rather than on the individual, evangelistic ministry was often considered a threat both to the religious institutions and to the state as well. Those who ventured to preach an authentic gospel were often executed, even in Protestant nations. The powers of this earth understood very well the threat that a true revival would be to them. Because of this, during the early 1700s there was almost universal opposition by both the political and ecclesiastical authorities to any kind of evangelical witness.

The birthing of the modern evangelical church—which was devoted to the value and the salvation of the individual—made the birth of modern democracy and the end of feudalism inevitable. **"Where the Spirit of the Lord is, there is liberty" (II Corinthians 3:17).** From Wycliff until the present time, even the world's most powerful governments were either transformed by the rising evangelical tide or washed away like sand castles before a great wave.

The political consequences of the Moravian movement were far-reaching, even though the Moravians never seemed to even consider such consequences important. The great democratic movements that began to spread around the world at that time are largely attributable to the biblical perspectives introduced by the Moravians. By keeping their focus on the kingdom of God and the spiritual consequences of their actions, the Moravians accomplished far more in the earthly realm than those in history who gave their whole attention to earthly matters.

It was directly through the Moravian influence on such spiritual titans as George

Whitfield and John and Charles Wesley that a repeat of the bloody French Revolution was kept from the shores of England. It was likewise through them that the seeds of the American Revolution were sown in the colonies, even though that was a purely unintentional result.

The primary seed which so powerfully impacted the world was simply the eternal value and dignity of the individual. When one is committed to the kingdom of God to the degree the Moravians were, the eternal destiny of an individual *far* outweighs anything that is temporary, including the whole world. As the Lord Himself stated, **"What will a man be profited, if he gains the whole world, and forfeits his soul?" (Matthew 16:26)** Ironically, those with this eternal perspective end up changing the world to a far greater degree than those whose devotion centers on resolving transitory world problems. Although it was said of Paul and Silas that they were turning the world upside down (Acts 17:6 KJV), they were really turning the world *right side up*.

THE FIRST MISSIONARIES

Regardless of the consequences, those who have experienced true conversion are the ones who cannot help but testify of the great grace of God which they have received. The hallmark of true Christian community is that it is not focused inwardly upon itself, but outwardly toward the enormous spiritual needs of the world. Just as the first result of the fall was for the man and woman to look at *themselves*, the first result of redemption is to get our eyes *off of ourselves*.

In fact, Christian maturity can generally be measured by the degree to which one has laid aside self-interest and given himself or herself to the interests of Christ. The genuineness of the spirituality at the Herrnhut community was evidenced by the fact that as they matured spiritually they became increasingly concerned about those who had never heard of the Savior.

By 1731 Zinzendorf had drifted almost entirely away from the affairs of state and had given himself to shepherding the Moravians at Herrnhut. Although he was not interested when he was invited to the coronation of Christian VI in Copenhagen, he submitted the matter to the congregation for prayer. The prevailing opinion was that he should go.

Although the Count was awarded the medal of the Order of the Danebrog for distinguished service, the special event for him during the coronation ceremonies was meeting Anthony Ulrich. Anthony was a black man who had been brought to Europe from St. Thomas, and he passionately pled for the Count to send someone to the West Indies to share the gospel with the slaves. The church existed there, but only for the whites.

The issue of missions had been burning in Zinzendorf's heart for some time, and he had encouraged a number of the young men at Herrnhut to study writing, geography, theology and medicine in order to be prepared for the day that they might be sent to other lands. When the Count recounted at Herrnhut his conversations with Anthony Ulrich in Copenhagen, two young men named Leonard Dober and Tobias Leupold were stirred to sleeplessness as they pondered the plight of the West Indies' slaves.

The next morning, as Dober opened his daily text of Scripture, he read, **"It is not a vain thing for you; because it is your life: and through this thing ye shall prolong your days" (Deuteronomy 32:47 KJV).** Dober was convinced that this was the Lord speaking to him about his growing desire to preach the gospel to the slaves in the West Indies. When he shared his thoughts with Leupold, he was amazed to find him thinking the same thing.

As these two young men were passing the Count's house that evening, they overheard him talking to a guest: "Sir, among these young men there are missionaries to St. Thomas, Greenland, Lapland and other countries." Astonished, they could barely contain their joy as they felt the Savior Himself speaking to them about their destiny. They immediately composed a letter to the Count, telling him of their intentions to go.

The Count shared the letter with the congregation without revealing its authors. Then Anthony Ulrich arrived at Herrnhut and repeated his plea to the congregation, which was greatly stirred. However, the wise Count knew better than to act too quickly. He submitted the desire of the two men to the congregation and then waited a number of months before allowing lots to be drawn for an answer. The lot for Leupold was "wait" but for Dober it stated "let the lad go." David Nitschmann, a carpenter, agreed to go with him. At an "unforgettable service" on August 18, 1731, the two men were commissioned and sent out by the congregation.

At 3:00 a.m. on the morning of August 21, the Count drove the two men in his own carriage to Bautzen. Outside the town, the three men got off the carriage. The Count laid his hands on Dober and blessed him with the simple instructions, "Do all in the spirit of Jesus Christ." Thus modern missions were born and "the golden decade" of the renewed Moravian Church began.

THE FIRES SPREAD

Over the next ten years, Moravian missionaries were sent to St. Croix, Greenland, Surinam, Guinea, South Africa, Lapland, Algeria, Ceylon, Romania, Constantinople (modern Istanbul), and North America. Out of the community of just 600, more than 70 had already been sent out by 1742.

The missionary fires spread, resulting in the persecution of the Count. He was banished from Saxony in 1736, but like the persecution of the first-century Christians, this only seemed to increase the flames. With Zinzendorf's banishment from Saxony, another Moravian community was founded in Hernhaag. Soon it had surpassed Herrnhut by sending out more than 200 missionaries in just one year. According to *Christian History* magazine, "The decade of 1732-42 stands unparalleled in Christian history insofar as missionary expansion is concerned."

In 1737 Zinzendorf was ordained a bishop in the Moravian Church by one of two surviving bishops, Daniel Ernest Jablonsky. The following year, the Count visited his missionaries on St. Thomas where he secured their freedom from prison, for they had been accused of preaching without a valid ordination. In 1741 he made his first visit to America, giving Bethlehem, Pennsylvania its name and strengthening the young congregation there. He also made extended trips to work among the Indians. While in America, Zinzendorf endeavored to unite the Protestant churches there, arguing that America did not yet have a history and therefore was not bound by the spiritual divisions of the European churches. His effort failed.

Because of Zinzendorf's commitment to Christian unity, the Moravian church never became a very large denomination. In fact, many of the congregations founded around the world were turned over to other denominations. New congregations were only allowed to remain a part of the Moravian fellowship if there was no other denomination to absorb them.

It could be argued that if it had not been for this noble practice, the modern Moravian church would be one of the largest denominations today. However, the legacy of the Moravian church was not meant to be just an institution, but a mighty demonstration of the power of God to change history by transforming men.

JOHN WESLEY ENCOUNTERS THE MORAVIANS

Countless men were transformed through the influence of the Moravians. When Jesus dwells in the heart of a man, that man contains a fire that will begin to burn in anyone else who is touched by it. When John Wesley was touched by the fire that burned in the Moravian missionary Spangenberg, he would never be the same. Wesley carried this fire back to England and from there cast it to every corner of the Empire.

During January 1736, Wesley was on a ship bound for America that also carried a number of Moravian missionaries. He was challenged by their great seriousness and their humility in performing for other passengers the most servile tasks, which none of the English passengers would do. When they were offered pay for this, they refused, replying that "it was good for their proud hearts," and "their loving Savior had done more for them." Some of the passengers abused them terribly, even striking them or knocking them down, yet they would never strike back or even take offense.

Many perceived these German missionaries as cowards until a great storm broke over the ship. As the main sail split and the sea began to pour into the ship, the English panicked, their terrified screams rising above the tumult of the storm. In contrast, the Moravians sat quietly, singing their hymns. Afterward, when one of the Moravians was asked if he was afraid during the storm, he answered, "I thank God, no." When he was asked if their women and children were afraid, and he replied, "No, our women and children are not afraid to die." Wesley recorded this in his diary and added:

> From them (the Moravians) I went to their crying, trembling neighbors, and pointed out to them the difference in the hour of trial, between him that feareth God, and him that feareth not. At twelve the wind fell. This was the most glorious

day which I have hitherto seen.

A month later, while in Savannah, Georgia, Wesley wrote:

> Mr. Delamotte and I took up our lodging with the Germans (the Moravians). We had now an opportunity, day by day, of observing their whole behavior. For we were in one room with them from morning to night...They were always employed, always cheerful themselves, and in good humor with one another; they had put away all anger and strife, and wrath, and bitterness, and clamor, and evil-speaking; they walked worthy of the vocation wherewith they were called, and adorned the Gospel of our Lord in all things.

John Wesley became especially attached to one of the Moravian leaders, Peter Böhler, and their paths crossed often in England after Wesley's return. Through Böhler, Wesley was impacted by the fact that even though he was an ordained clergyman, he did not have true saving faith in Christ. This sent Wesley into a period of great personal grief, consternation and seeking.

Wesley's encounters with Böhler and the letters he received from him were always timely, keeping Wesley focused on his quest for true faith. Even though Böhler was much younger than he, Wesley would later refer to this gentle but resolute Moravian missionary as his spiritual father.

A HEART "STRANGELY WARMED"

As John Wesley searched the Scriptures, he found continual conflict between what he had been taught and the literal interpretation of the Word of God. He knew that he could not hold on to both—he had to embrace one or the other. He was also tormented by the fact that he did not have the "personal experience and assurance" of salvation spoken of in the Scriptures. After yet another visit from Böhler and two of his companions, Wesley resolved to believe the Scriptures and "seek the grace of God until the end."

Wesley's new commitment to seek the grace of God was not some religious platitude that he had no intention of fulfilling. His journal records the specific approach that he was devoting himself to:

1. Absolutely renouncing all dependence, in whole or in part, upon my own works or righteousness; on which I had really grounded my hope of salvation, though I knew it not, from my youth up.

2. Adding to the constant use of all the other means of grace, continual

prayer for this very thing justifying, saving faith, a full reliance on the blood of Christ shed for *me*; a trust in Him, as *my* Christ, as *my* sole justification, sanctification and redemption.

After making this resolution, Wesley opened his New Testament and his eyes fell on the words of II Peter 1:4 (KJV): **"Whereby are given unto us exceeding great and precious promises: that by these ye might be partakers of the divine nature, having escaped the corruption that is in the world through lust."** Later in the day he opened it again and saw the words, **"Thou art not far from the kingdom of God" (Mark 12:34 KJV)**. Feeling that the Lord had personally spoken to him through these scriptures, Wesley remarked later that even the hymns sung at St. Paul's that day seemed to be personal messages to him.

That evening, while sitting at the Aldersgate-Street Society and listening to someone read Luther's preface to his commentary on Romans, Wesley recorded the now famous words, "I felt my heart strangely warmed. I felt I did trust in Christ, Christ alone for salvation. And an assurance was given me that He had taken away *my* sins, even *mine,* and saved *me* from the law of sin and death."

The Moravians themselves have never been credited with nation-sweeping and history-changing revivals such as Luther and the Wesley brothers sparked. However, the revival seeds they sowed can be traced throughout history, as many who encountered the Moravians would in turn light widespread spiritual fires. The conversion of John Wesley is typical of the historic Moravian style of ministry—to remain hidden and small, but have such an impact on their times that it would be impossible to imagine what history would be like without them.

The Moravians themselves were never revivalists. Rather, they were spiritual plodders who spent themselves breaking up the fallow ground so that others could plant and reap. While Wesley and Whitfield were seeing thousands come to Christ in their meetings, some of the Moravian missionary outposts were suffering the death of one missionary for every soul saved.

Although most who travel today's highways never give a thought to the engineers and workers who cut the difficult path inch-by-inch through underbrush, forest, wilderness and mountains, our way is made possible only by their labor. As Isaiah observed, **"A**

voice is calling, 'Clear the way for the Lord in the wilderness; make smooth in the desert a highway for our God'" (Isaiah **40:3).** Like the Moravians, many have struggled through the most inhospitable spiritual wildernesses to make a highway for those who would come after them. Today we cruise along over spiritual territory that was paid for by the blood, the sweat, and the lives of those who took up their crosses daily and made sacrifice a way of life.

In his later years, Zinzendorf sometimes lived in tents with Indians and trekked over dangerous terrain, spending his entire life and fortune seeking to reach those who had never heard the gospel. He and his Moravian comrades often went where others were not willing to go.

Without fanfare or dramatic revivals, the Moravians possibly impacted history more during the past 500 years than any other single spiritual or political force. But their influence will not be confined to the past. This faithful group, dubbed by Hus as "the hidden seed," has also undoubtedly planted many more seeds still to be reaped in the harvest at the end of the age.

AUTHOR'S NOTE

This is but a superficial and incomplete outline of the great story of the Moravians. My objective has been only to stir the readers to a more in-depth study of these powerful and inspirational histories. Following are the main sources of my study for this article:

Count Zinzendorf by John R. Weinlick

The Moravian Church Through the Ages by John R. Weinlick

Power from on High by John Greenfield

All About the Moravians by Edwin A. Sawyer

Hidden Seed and Harvest by Chester S. Davis

All of these books are distributed by The Moravian Church in America, 500 South Church Street, Winston-Salem, NC 27101.

Another important source for this booklet was ***Christian History*** magazine, whose inaugural issue featured Zinzendorf and the Moravians in honor of the 250th anniversary of Protestant missions. I consider ***Christian History*** to be one of the most important and well done Christian periodicals being published today. A subscription to this magazine can be obtained from **Christian History, P.O. Box 11631, Des Moines, IA 50340-1631**. Back issues, including the issue devoted to Zinzendorf and the Moravians, are also available.

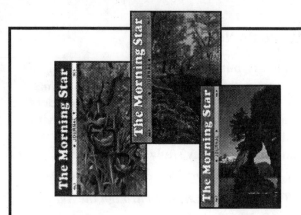